UNBROKEN CIRCLE

UNBROKEN CIRCLE

A QUOTABLE HISTORY OF THE GRAND OLE OPRY

Compiled and Edited by
Randall Bedwell

CUMBERLAND HOUSE
Nashville, Tennessee

Published by Cumberland House Publishing, Inc., 431 Harding Industrial Drive, Nashvillle, Tennessee 37211

Cover design by Unlikely Suburban Design.

Some quotes have been edited for clarity and brevity.

Library of Congress Cataloging-in-Publication Data

Unbroken circle: : a quotable history of the Grand Ole Opry / compiled
    and edited by Randall Bedwell.
        p.   cm.
    Includes bibliographical references.
    ISBN: 1-58182-014-3
    1. Grand Ole Opry (Radio program)—History quotations, maxims,
etc. 2. Country musicians—United States Quotations. I. Bedwell,
Randall J.
    ML68.U8   1999
    791.44'72—dc21   99-41844
                                                             CIP

CONTENTS

UNBROKEN CIRCLE

INTRODUCTION

"Will the Circle Be Unbroken" was the last song performed on the night of the Grand Ole Opry's final show at the old Ryman Auditorium on March 15, 1974. The radio broadcast had already been concluded when Johnny Cash led a round of gospel hymns.

"Will the Circle Be Unbroken" was also the first song performed on the premier broadcast of a televised special from Opryland USA after the Grand Ole Opry's move there.

The most dramatic symbol linking the Ryman with Opryland is a circle cut from the wooden stage at the former and installed at the latter. Any time performers take the stage at the new Opryland today, they do so on the same circle where the immortals of country music stood before them.

From Uncle Dave Macon to Patsy Cline and Roy Acuff to Hank Williams, the storied past of the Grand Ole Opry lives on.

Unbroken Circle: A Quotable History of the Grand Ole Opry is a tribute to the greatest comments in the history of this most homegrown of American institutions.

The Grand Ole Opry is a name synonymous with country music. It

9

is the oldest radio and stage show in history—a radio show like no other in the annals of broadcasting.

The circle remains unbroken.

—Randall Bedwell

CHAPTER ONE

IN THE BEGINNING

While urban America in 1925 was enjoying the prosperity of post-World War I expansion, many cotton farmers, coal miners, and textile workers were experiencing a different fate. Poverty remained entrenched in the Great Smoky Mountains, the Appalachians, and the Ozarks.

With the advent and development of improved and accessible communications technology during the twentieth century, city and country lifestyles crept toward each other. In the most remote regions of rural America in 1925, however, significant cultural differences endured. Nowhere was this more evident than in music. Rural Americans composed their own tunes to the accompaniment of fiddles, banjos, and guitars. Their songs spoke from the heart of hard times; of love, both true and untrue; and of a faith in God unshaken by modern science.

Once radios became commonplace, a market developed for this homespun music. At first it was called hillbilly music, but it later became known simply as country.

Nashville was actually an unlikely site to become the capital of country music. In 1925, Tennessee's state capital boasted a symphony, a downtown skyline comprised of tall buildings filled with white-collar workers, and even a shining replica of the ancient Greek Parthenon. In fact, city leaders liked to call Nashville "the Athens of the South."

Nashville radio station WSM went on the air in October 1925—a result of National Life and Accident Insurance Company executive Edwin Craig's belief that it would be an ideal vehicle for promoting insurance sales. "WSM—We Serve Millions" was the company slogan.

Craig recognized radio's ability to reach all of the potential customers that company salesmen were calling on, both in the city and out in the countryside. When Craig launched WSM, its early broadcasts featured mostly classical music. But it would be country that soon made WSM famous.

The WSM Barn Dance began as one of many barn-dance programs in the 1920s featuring country folk tunes, but it was the only one that would endure and become an American icon.

At 8:00 P.M. on Saturday, November 28, 1925, the WSM Barn Dance was first broadcast under that name. The host was George Hay, an announcer who had gotten his start in Memphis and had long called himself "the Solemn Old Judge" on the radio.

That first show featured eighty-year-old fiddler Uncle Jimmy Thompson, who had learned many of his tunes during the Civil War. He was an immediate hit. The show lasted one hour, although within two years it was lengthened into a three-hour program and made into a Saturday-night tradition for countless listeners.

Early performers were not musicians by profession—just farmers, mechanics, and other workers whose hobby was music. Hay gave them colorful names such as the Crook Brothers, Uncle Ed Poplin and his Ole Timers, the Gully Jumpers, the Fruit Jar Drinkers, and the Possum

Hunters. Uncle Dave Macon, a banjo-picking storyteller known as "the Dixie Dewdrop," emerged as WSM's first big star.

The Barn Dance became known as the Grand Ole Opry in 1927. That's when Hay spontaneously coined the name, inspired by a symphony broadcast that preceded it on WSM. The new name helped distinguish the show from all other barn-dance broadcasts on other radio stations. In the popular imagination, what WSM presented wasn't just another barn dance. There was only one Grand Ole Opry.

It will be down to earth for the earthy.
—GEORGE HAY, first host of the WSM Barn Dance

Why shucks, a man don't get warmed up in an hour. I just won an eight-day fiddling contest down in Dallas.
—UNCLE JIMMY THOMPSON, eighty-year-old fiddler jesting at the end of the first WSM Barn Dance broadcast, on November 28, 1925

We were outstanding in our field. And that's where they found us—out standing in the field.
—KIRK McGEE, early Opry musician

For the past hour, we have been listening to music taken largely from grand opera. But from now on, we will present the Grand Ole Opry.

—GEORGE HAY, contrasting the WSM Barn Dance with a preceding symphony broadcast in 1927 and coining the name the show has been known by ever since

To lay it on the line like it was, Judge Hay didn't know music; he couldn't memorize tunes. He wouldn't know the difference between "Turkey in the Straw" and "Steamboat Bill." He liked rapid tunes because he thought the man that was making the most racket was making the most music.

—Anonymous interviewee, in the *Journal of Country Music,* quoted by Richard A. Peterson and Paul Di Maggio

Before making it to the Ryman, the early Grand Ole Opry bounced between several locales, including the Dixie Tabernacle, as pictured here in 1936. (Photo courtesy of Country Music Hall of Fame)

We're nothing but a bunch of hillbillies from North Carolina and Virginia. Call us anything.
                        —AL HOPKINS, member of the Hill Billies,
                              responding in 1925 to a question
                              about what to call his group

We tried "producing it," and we almost ruined it.... You've never seen anything so stilted in your life as the time when we decided to have a script, with set entrances and lines that had to be learned.
                                    —EDWIN CRAIG

Each Saturday night brought more than its quota of people who wanted to watch our broadcast. They milled around for several hours and most of them stuck to the finish. They were hungry for the rhythm of the soil and the heart songs, plus the rural flavor and humor which spiced it.

—GEORGE HAY

It is much more difficult to comprehend the success of a radio show than to understand the success of a singer, a song, or a record.... To a certain degree one can never hope to understand why the Opry became popular in its first five years simply because no one will ever be able to listen to an Opry program from that period. Yet this intangible element (the radio Opry) was apparently a prime force in the popularization and development of country music.

—CHARLES K. WOLFE, writing in the *Journal of Country Music*

I don't know anything about those hillbillies, and I don't want anything to do with that show.

—VITO PELLETTIERI, a former orchestra leader, before becoming stage manager of the Opry for almost forty years

The rougher he talked to you, the better he liked you.

—Anonymous performer, on Pellettieri

WSM had a good-natured riot on its hands.

—GEORGE HAY on the stunningly rapid popularity of the WSM Barn Dance

George Hay onstage at the Opry with Kitty Wells, in the early fifties. (Photo courtesy of Country Music Hall of Fame)

We played for two years for nothin'. But we didn't think much about that, because back there then, you see, radio was something new and we were just tickled to say that we got to play over the radio.

—HERMAN CROOK, early Opry harmonica player
who became a longtime regular

The station regrets that it cannot invite the general public to be present at the studio.... but in order that those who have no receiving sets who desire to hear the program can do so, the Western Electric Company will install large loud-speakers in windows of the National building, and as many as care to can assemble in front of the building and enjoy the broadcast.

—WSM newspaper advertisement for the station's opening

Mr. Craig became a long-distance radio enthu-
siast, or DX fan, as the hams call it. DX fans were
people who could sit up all night listening to people around the country talk on the radio. It got
Mr. Craig very excited.

—JACK DEWITT JR.

Opry stars would frequently make one hundred
one-nighters in a year, speeding over back roads
to fairgrounds, tent shows, National Guard
armories, onstage in Rochester, or Detroit, dri-
ving all night to return in time for the next
Saturday Opry performance. The musicians were
paid little for their radio work, and out of finan-
cial necessity had to bolster record sales with
whirlwind forays into the hinterlands.

—JOHN SCOTT COLLEY, writing in the
Journal of Country Music

Now we'll show you how Uncle Dave handles a banjo like a monkey handles a peanut!

—GEORGE HAY, introducing Uncle Dave Macon
at an Opry performance

To say I had become an Opry fan would be putting it mildly. All week long I waited for Saturday night so I could tune in to WSM.

—ROY ACUFF, remembering his boyhood
fascination with the show

Uncle Dave Macon having and showing a good time, flanked by his son Dorris and Cousin Rachàel. (Photo courtesy of Country Music Hall of Fame)

My first memory of the Grand Ole Opry was on my grandfather's farm [in Baxter] in the mid to late forties. We didn't have electricity on Granddad's farm. He had an old, dry-cell, battery-operated radio that he wouldn't allow Grandmother to turn on, except for about five minutes in the morning. She'd get to hear the news, then it was cut off until Saturday night and the Grand Ole Opry.

—BOB WHITTAKER, Opry general manager

The [1928 Grand Ole Opry] show was more tightly programmed and less casual than usually imagined. There was also more variety and less pure old-time music than usually believed.... Hay's Opry of 1928 was more hillbilly in its image than in fact and represents an important stage in the transformation of old-time music into commercial country music.

—from the *Journal of Country Music*

Roy Acuff, here flanked by his Smoky Mountain Boys in the early 1940s, was a Grand Ole Opry legend for more than half a century. (Photo courtesy of Country Music Hall of Fame)

Radio in general and the Grand Ole Opry in particular got a whole lot of people through the depression.

—ROY ACUFF

[A hillbilly sings] more sincere than most entertainers because the hillbilly was raised rougher than most entertainers. You got to know a lot about hard work.

—HANK WILLIAMS

I'll tell you, we got a lot of our pickin' from the colored people.... They played some real chords. They didn't know what they were an' we didn't either. Still don't.

—KIRK MCGEE

What would great down-home Opry music be without some onstage hoofers?
(Photo courtesy of Country Music Hall of Fame)

CHAPTER TWO

THE RYMAN

Long before the Ryman Auditorium became the shrine of country music, it began, appropriately, as a house of God.

The Grand Ole Opry was almost twenty years old by the time it found its way to the Ryman. In its early years, the Opry had various homes, including the National Life and Accident Insurance Company building, a former movie theater, a former revival house, and then the War Memorial Auditorium as the crowds kept growing.

The Opry relocated to the Ryman Auditorium in downtown Nashville in 1941, and that's where the Opry stayed and gained a foothold of fame before it was relocated to Opryland USA in the early 1970s.

The Ryman had been built in 1889. Tough, rowdy riverboat owner Thomas Ryman resolved to undertake the project after hearing fire-and-brimstone, nineteenth-century revivalist Samuel Jones preach against iniquity in Nashville. Ryman, who had made his fortune transporting whiskey and operating casinos on his steamboats, became a changed man.

Ryman told Jones he was going to build a tabernacle for all denominations. The result was the Union Gospel Tabernacle, later renamed the Ryman Auditorium.

Construction costs were so great that Ryman was still paying off his debts at the time of his death in 1904. The building featured a red-brick, white-trimmed exterior, Gothic windows, and a rounded interior that was both grand and intimate. The first revival was held in 1890, even before construction was complete.

Over the years the auditorium was opened to secular activities, hosting orators such as William Jennings Bryan and Booker T. Washington, the Nashville symphony and opera, political conventions, and performers ranging from Rudolph Valentino to W. C. Fields to Mary Pickford.

And then came the Opry. Where evangelist Billy Sunday had once warned, "Repent!" Minnie Pearl would warble, "How-deee!"

For some reason that stage at the Ryman takes precedence over everything else. It's almost hallowed ground, so to speak, when you think back to Hank Williams, George Morgan, Patsy Cline, Marty Robbins—people no longer with us.

—JEANNE PRUETT

We all know [the Ryman] was built as a tabernacle, and I would cry sometimes when I heard Anita [Carter]'s pure, sweet voice in that old building. It was just like hearing an angel sing.

—DOTTIE WEST

Dottie West has long been a class act. (ICM file photo provided by Lomax Photo Archives)

It still has that magic about the sound of it. It's unbelievable. A guy told me one time that the old building was like the inside of a great acoustic guitar: the wood was dry and it had its own sound. I think that's true.

—PORTER WAGONER, commenting on the Opry's return for a special performance at the Ryman in January 1999.

Sometimes cool air wasn't the only thing that came in (due to the lack of air conditioning). I was on the stage down there one night in the middle of summertime, and some kinda great ol' bug flew right down my throat. That's when they started calling me "Whisperin' Bill."... Ernest Tubb's bass player leaned over to me and said, "Let the bug sing."

—BILL ANDERSON, recalling an embarrassing moment at the Ryman

It was like a singer's dream heaven. Although the old Ryman was hot and uncomfortable, it had such a friendliness to it. Everybody loved everybody.

—MARTHA CARSON, singer

And then when they told me about how that circle in the middle of the stage came from the old Ryman Auditorium, I could really feel the history and the emotion that all the Opry members share.

—CLINT BACK

The Ryman is like a fine instrument; it's aged. It's a place that musicians want to play because of the sound.

—NEIL DIAMOND, who first performed at the Ryman in 1972

For many years, unbeknownst
to the Opry's final-segment host
Marty Robbins, WSM radio listeners were
hearing a show closing different from what the
live audience at the Ryman was experiencing.
The Opry had pretaped a closing for Robbins's
radio segment, even though Robbins would
continue performing for his live audience
after WSM had already switched to other
programming. "We'd punch in this closing
of him singing 'El Paso' and the sign-off, but
it just went to the radio audience," Hal
Durham explained. "Here in the house they
were still seeing a Marty Robbins concert.
He could go another thirty minutes.
We finally told him what we
were doing. He didn't realize
it, but he didn't mind."

It made my head swim to see all those hand fans a-pumpin' out there. I'd get so dizzy I'd have to close my eyes.

—ROY ACUFF, referring to the hand fans sold
at the Ryman on warm nights

This is a nice place to visit, but I sure wouldn't want to sit here.

—Anonymous Opry-goer, referring to the hard pews in the Ryman

Get your fans—25 cents. The Ryman is *not* air-conditioned. You will drownded in yo' own sweat!

–Anonymous young boy sellng Opry-goers in line
on a hot summer evening in 1972

A packed house at the Ryman was a common occurrence for decades. (Photo courtesy of Country Music Hall of Fame)

The Ryman remains the most amazing place I've ever sung in. The acoustics, the way the music reverberates and decays, is so perfect.

—VINCE GILL

The cheapest seats were always there under the balcony. And you'd have popcorn and stuff falling on your head, and if somebody spilled a Coke, it would leak on your head. At least I hope it was a Coke.

—LORETTA LYNN

Most of us came to work dressed, because there was no place to change.

—LITTLE JIMMY DICKENS, commenting on the cramped space Opry members endured from 1943 to 1974 at the Ryman

More like accidental organization.
> —JEANNIE SEELY, when asked if the frenzied activity backstage
> at the Ryman could be described as organized chaos

When I get up to preach, I just knock out the bung and let nature cut her capers.
> —SAM JONES, Georgia evangelist who had a profound spiritual
> effect on Nashville riverboat captain Tom Ryman
> in the late nineteenth century

I realize that those are penitential seats you're sitting in.
> —GARRISON KEILLOR, to the audience when the Ryman was
> reopened for live performances in June 1994, with his
> *Prairie Home Companion* on the bill that night

The polished wooden pews sat glistening in the afternoon sun that filtered through the windows and gave the aroma of a thousand old guitars. There's nothing else like it. It makes you hungry for good music.

—TOM T. HALL

The devil's backbone.

—BILLY SUNDAY, evangelist, preaching at the Ryman in pre-World War II days, referring to lower Broadway and Nashville's red-light district

The Ryman was a church before it was the Mother Church of Country Music, so we thought it was a perfect place to blend the spiritual side with the music.

—TRISHA YEARWOOD, referring to her 1994 marriage to the Mavericks' Robert Reynolds at the Ryman

Crowds were lining up outside the Ryman hours before the start of the next Opry show. (Les Leverett photo)

I am honored to work and play there and call it my home. More importantly, I call the people I work with there my friends. The decades of those kinds of relationships echo off the walls of that glorious old building and resound in a special place in my heart.

—GARY CHAPMAN, host of "Sam's Place—Music for the Spirit," taped at the Ryman

I love that old building. I love the feeling it gives me, and I love the people.

—JOHNNY CASH

There were some nice things about the old Ryman. I remember, for instance, some tables to the left of the stage where we used to sit and talk and laugh and relax. In the earlier days, Robert Lunn used to hold court there. He was one of our favorite comedians. He used to get a lot of laughs by telling all these guys who managed to sneak backstage and try to get on the show that he was the one in charge of giving auditions. A lot of times he would take them out in the alley and make them dance or juggle or some such thing that had nothing at all to do with their singing.

—GRANDPA JONES

Grandpa Jones, Roy Acuff, and Little Jimmy Dickens each spent many years performing at the Ryman. (Photo provided by Lomax Photo Archives)

You know what I recall most about the old Ryman? It's dressing and getting made up and all in the toilet, which was the women's dressing room. Sharing that crowded space with Loretta Lynn and Connie Smith and Dolly Parton and Jeannie Seely.

—BARBARA MANDRELL

If they'd just give me the Ryman back with its dust and paint, and a big block of tickets, I wouldn't ask anything else.

—LULA NAFF, Ryman general manager 1920–1955

You just don't know how much we do appreciate you people. It's you who have made the Grand Ole Opry so successful. Will you not forget us when we move into our new building? You'll love us for being out there, and we'll love you for coming to see us. Thank you. God bless you all—good night.

—ROY ACUFF, in his final Ryman show

That's how the older members of the Opry got to know each other.

—JEANNIE SEELY, on the Ryman's lack of privacy backstage

I have dreamed of singing on this stage. How wonderful to be a part of a place that honors not only where we are going—who we are becoming—but celebrates where we have been and all that we come from.

—AMY GRANT

I think it was a fitting tribute to our dad.

—JETT WILLIAMS, commenting on meeting her brother, Hank Jr. for the first time on the seventy-fifth anniversary of the legendary singer Hank Williams's birthday with the unveiling of a statue in his honor. The statue now sits in the lobby of the Grand Ole Opry.

Before I ever came to the Grand Ole Opry, I had a better dressing room than this. And it was a crapper, too.

—PATSY CLINE

It is a sign of a good civilization for cities to preserve and maintain historic areas such as the Ryman Auditorium.

—CASPER WEINBERGER, former U.S. defense secretary

America's most picturesque institution.

—BOB HOPE, who appeared at the Ryman in 1949

We couldn't believe we were there, standing on the same stage and playing and singing through the same microphone as all those great artists we'd heard on the radio even before we started playing music.

—ALISON KRAUSS

[Porter Wagoner] would take me over to the Opry, and of course I got to meet Dolly [Parton] through his television show. Dolly was wonderful. I remember a time at the old Ryman when Dolly would go to the ladies' room backstage and show me how to put on makeup.

—PATTY LOVELESS, who met Porter Wagoner in 1971, when she was fourteen

The audience is much closer at the Ryman than at the Opry House. There's a little more magnetism to it. You communicate better. Seems like the Ryman audiences were into it a little more.

—BILL ANDERSON, when asked about the
differences between Opry venues

It's going to be all right.

—MINNIE PEARL, through tears in 1974 at the
Opry's final show at the Ryman

CHAPTER THREE

THE FIRST TIME

Making one's debut at the Grand Ole Opry has always been an unforgettable, even unnerving, experience for hundreds of performers covering numerous decades. For most performers, stepping into the circle is a moment they have dreamed about and worked toward for many years.

Sometimes it goes well: A star is born. Sometimes the jitters are overwhelming. Sometimes the moment takes on the qualities of a vision or even a religious experience. Some performers have talked of feeling the presence of singers, pickers, and other legendary performers long since gone, while others have claimed an inexplicable warmth or chills that they have never had on any other stage.

Regardless of the symptoms felt, if any, going onstage at the Opry for the first time can be an intimidating venture. Like a first kiss, a first car, or a first child, it's something beyond comparison with almost any other event in one's life.

They were scared of me. They didn't think I was country. They said, "The Grand Ole Opry will go to any extent to keep from having anybody think that we're putting a phony up, and we're afraid they'll think you're a phony."

—MINNIE PEARL, recalling her 1940 audition
for the Grand Ole Opry

Well, we nearly dropped! It was hard to believe. There we were talking to Roy Acuff!

—PATSY CLINE

Patsy Cline's days at the Opry were far too few. (ICM file photo provided by Lomax Photo Archives)

I went down and auditioned for Judge Hay, and he left me standing there and said he'd be back in a minute. I thought he was going after that guard to put me in that elevator! But he brought Dee Kilpatrick with him. I sang three songs. They said, "Follow us." He opened a drawer, pulled a contract out, and said, "Put your name right here." I saw it, and it said something like "regular member, five-year contract." So, of course, that's been all I've ever signed.

—STONEWALL JACKSON, on his audition for the Opry

I was invited to Nashville to perform on the Grand Ole Opry. For a month I was briefed as though I were going to a foreign country and should know all the rules of protocol.

—MARGARET WHITING, singer

My little 13-year-old knees were absolutely knocking, but I saw Dad standing there just bawling, and those people gave me a standing ovation. I thought "This is what I'm doing the rest of my life."

—LORRIE MORGAN, on her first Opry appearance

My knees started knocking, and I felt like I was doing my first talent contest, even though I had ten years' experience.

—LITTLE JIMMY DICKENS, recalling his first Opry performance

I guess I never was more scared than I was the night I replaced Roy Acuff.... The people thought I was a Chicago slicker who had come to pass himself off as a country boy and bump Roy out of his job.

—RED FOLEY

Jan Howard insisted on giving up her spot on the show for me and I was stunned.... I remember saying, "I can't do this, I'm just wearing jeans." The next thing I knew, I was being carried on stage by Jerry Clower! I think I sang "Delta Dawn." I don't really remember because I was so overwhelmed by the whole experience. I do know that my heart was full of love for Jan and Jerry and the rest of the Opry family. I was so proud to be there.

—TANYA TUCKER

There was a time early in her career that Minnie Pearl wondered if she would even pass her Opry audition. (Photo provided by Lomax Photo Archives)

I was twenty-eight, but I might as well have been sixteen. I had never been on the radio, and I was frightened completely out of my gourd.

—MINNIE PEARL, on her Opry debut

One of my dreams when I was a young man was to be on the Opry. I hit a lot of side tracks but never lost that desire, and now that I've got my act together in my later years, it's so great to walk out on that stage and be part of a great tra-dition.

—JOHNNY PAYCHECK, inducted into the Opry
in November 1997

I have never been so scared of going on stage.... When I got in that circle, it was like all the ghosts of the former Opry stars were standing in that circle with me. It was like they were saying, "Okay, this is our house and here is your chance. What are you going to do with it?" It was really an eerie feeling.

—SAMMY KERSHAW

I talk to the newcomers before they go out on that stage. I tell them that I don't want to be able to see anything but their backs and when they come off I want them to be able to recognize anybody in that audience if they ever see them again.

—VITO PELLETTIERI, Opry stage manager
from 1934 for almost forty years

I bought my first rhinestone suit in 1951, as soon as I had the money to get one. It was orange with blue wagons on it, and the first time I ever sang on the Grand Ole Opry I wore it. By the time I retired it, the sequins wouldn't even shine any more. It was a thread-bare bastard.

—PORTER WAGONER

All other achievements pale in comparison. It's the only place where I still get nervous and still get cotton mouth.

—JOE DIFFIE, who joined the Opry in 1993

Hank Snow's debut at the Opry didn't go very well, but he made up for lost time in a hurry. (RCA Records file photo provided by Lomax Photo Archives)

I don't mind telling you that I bombed. The people just sat there while I sang. No applause, no nothing. Just sat.

—HANK SNOW

A bunch of them would come up in their overalls and straw hats, holding their instruments, and I'd ask them what they called themselves, and they'd say they didn't call themselves anything. So I'd have to holler over at the Judge and say, "What do you want to name this bunch, Mr. Hay?" and he'd say, "Aw, let's call them the Gully Jumpers ... or the Fruit Jar Drinkers ... or something." That's the way the Fruit Jar Drinkers got named.

—VITO PELLETTIERI, Opry stage manager since 1934

My first show was with Ernest Tubb. I was scared. I didn't have real good clothes, I just had some khakis and they were patched and a little frail. When I went on that night, I had that old guitar with my name on it with fingernail polish. The musicians thought they'd hired another comedian. When Ernest put me on, the backup pickers were laughing. The audience was laughing, too. The song I sang was "Don't Be Angry." It's not a joking song and the audience got real quiet and the guys on stage got real quiet. I encored about four times. That was my first taste of having applause.

—STONEWALL JACKSON, member of the Opry since 1956

Appearing on NBC's Prince Albert portion of the Opry, hosted by Roy Acuff and broadcast nationwide, [Ernest] Tubb—in spite of his nervousness—was an immediate hit with the Opry fans. He was called back for three encores of his hit "Walking the Floor Over You." He learned of the encores only when Oscar Davis later told him about them. Tubb was simply too scared to remember what had happened on stage.

—RONNIE PUGH, writing in the *Journal of Country Music*

I was right in that mike, just whippin' it on, just the best I could do it, with all my heart. And that audience seen how serious I was, and they just got quiet. And I encored four times. I guess an older man might have had a heart attack.

—STONEWALL JACKSON, on his first Opry appearance

The thing that surprised me most was how right it felt. Once I got onstage and started doing my song, it was kind of like I belonged there. The people had a way of making you feel you belonged.

—PORTER WAGONER

I remember playing with Patty Loveless the night she was inducted, and that was one of the highlights of my life. I know some people think it's old hat, but whenever one of our acts plays the Opry for the first time, I like to see how they do, because to me it's just another barometer of how they fare with a really hard-core country music audience.

—TONY BROWN, MCA Nashville president
and himself a musician

The first time I performed on the Opry, I was so nervous. But I remembered the advice that Judge Hay had given Minnie Pearl the first time she was on the Opry. He told her to love the audience and they'd love her right back. I thought that was a great perspective and that has always stuck with me.

—CLINT BLACK

I came off and asked my mamma, "How do you think it went?" And she said, "Several people woke up."

—MINNIE PEARL

I don't think I even got out "Doodle-do-do-do-do," which was my trademark, before I started crying. Porter Wagoner came up and put his arms around me. And when he done that, I laid my head on his shoulder, and the band kept playing, and Porter started getting tears in his eyes, and it was just one big crying mess.

—DEL REEVES, on the night he achieved his lifelong ambition of appearing on the Grand Ole Opry

I remember going out onstage and I remember tapping my foot. I was so scared I don't remember anything else.

—LORETTA LYNN

Boxcar Willie was practically a senior citizen by the time he made his Opry debut. (Photo provided by Lomax Photo Archives)

I looked out, and I swear to God I saw my mamma! Standing there, smiling. I mean, I didn't see her, but in my mind I knew she was there. A dream, you know. I promised Mamma—I guess I was probably ten—that someday I would be on the Opry.

—BOXCAR WILLIE, on the night he finally made his debut on the Opry, at the age of forty-nine

I hope I can carry on with what you and the rest of the Opry members have done over the years, because you and everybody else that belongs to the Opry, you are country music.

—RICKY VAN SHELTON, at his Opry debut, after being introduced by Roy Acuff

My family has always had the dream, and I have always had the dream to be a member of the Opry. And now they've accepted me and the music that I do and have made me a part of the Opry family.

—PATTY LOVELESS, at her first Opry appearance

The Opry was the only place in the world that made me nervous.

—RICKY SKAGGS

When I walked onto that stage for the first time, I was in the middle of singing "Killin' Time," and I could feel Hank Williams and Ernest Tubb. I still get goosebumps just thinking about it.

—CLINT BLACK

I am grateful, happy, and humble. It's the ambition of every hillbilly singer to reach the Opry in his lifetime. I feel mighty lucky to be here tonight.

—JOHNNY CASH, to the audience on the night
he made his Opry debut

I guess it's pretty much like if you're a politician and you get to walk into the Oval Office and sit behind the president's desk for two or three seconds. You know you're sitting where all the greats have sat.

—T. G. SHEPPARD, on what it's like to play the Opry
for the first time

The first time I sang there, the heat went all through my body when I started singing. It was definitely a spiritual vibe, an awesome feeling.

—VINCE GILL

I guess, outside of my marriage, that was the biggest event in my life.
—DOLLY PARTON, on her first appearance on the real Opry

They said, "You can't be on the Opry. You're not in the union." I said, "What's a union?"
—DOLLY PARTON, on her eventually successful efforts as a twelve-year-old to sing on a Friday-night version of the Opry

I bought a box of cigars and threw them off the stage.
—TENNESSEE ERNIE FORD, who made his debut Opry appearance just after learning that his first son had been born

CHAPTER FOUR

THE POWER

The prestige and influence of the Grand Ole Opry can be staggering. Time and time again, it has demonstrated its power to make stars, change lives, and cast a spell over its audience.

The Opry opened doors and generated business for its sponsors. It made household names of country pickers and singers. It spun lasting dreams in countless hearts touched by its Saturday night broadcasts.

The Opry was the centerpiece of the modern economy of Nashville, which was built on the twin pillars of tourism and the record industry. The Opry created a national consumer market for country music, thus forming the foundation for today's boom in country music.

The power and influence of the Opry lives on.

Being a member of the Grand Ole Opry is not really like an achievement to me. It's not like winning an award or selling a million albums. It's personal for me. You can't win it and you can't buy it and all the promoters in the world can't convince somebody to do it.

—CLINT BLACK

Country music is a format that hangs onto the lyric and I think the lyric is becoming everyday life. It's the ten o'clock news put to music. And I think that people are looking for something to learn from.

—GARTH BROOKS

You got to remember, kid, that one broadcast on the Grand Ole Opry means twenty weeks' work somewhere else.

—PEE WEE KING, bandleader of the Golden West Cowboys,
on advice given him by his agent

The Opry to a country singer is what Yankee Stadium is to a baseball player or Hollywood is to an actor or an actress or what Broadway is to somebody in the theater. It's the pinnacle. It's the highest you can go. It's the greatest honor that can be bestowed upon somebody in our field of music.... It's by invitation. It's nothing you can earn. You've got to be invited, and I think that's very special.

—BILL ANDERSON

"Whispering" Bill Anderson made some tasty biscuits when he wasn't hosting "Backstage at the Grand Ole Opry." (Photo provided by Lomax Photo Archives)

The Opry is a good platform for the politicians if they're in town.... It's one of the stops if you're running for president.

—CHARLIE WALKER, Opry star

It has grown, and we've seen the evolution in its form. I suppose it had to change, but in the early years it gave a start to many, many singers and pickers. It came to be the dream of every folk musician to be on the Opry.

—EDWIN CRAIG, creator of the Grand Ole Opry

If it hadn't been for the Opry, I think I might have fallen by the wayside, because I don't think I would have ever really become known.

—ROY ACUFF

I've always loved country music ever since I was a kid. Living in a small rural town in the South, we kids were in bed by eight o'clock. But my mom would let me stay up on Saturday night, 'cause she knew I loved the Grand Ole Opry. That was the only time I got to stay up till ten o'clock, just to hear that one program.

—RAY CHARLES

Ray Charles was raised on the music of the Grand Ole Opry. (Photo provided by Lomax Photo Archives)

This, of course, was the Opry influence.
—IRVING WAUGH, WSM president, on how one of the first-ever
national radio surveys showed that as early as 1948,
WSM was reaching an astounding audience
of more than ten million homes

Somebody said, "The circle still lives." I think that's important, because you can almost see hesitancy every time a new artist walks on stage and they take that step—that step that actually steps on that circle where all of the greats have stood. I think it's that part of this venue and this show that continues to make people want to come in.
—BOB WHITTAKER, Opry general manager

I didn't realize that the centerpiece I was standing on was from the Ryman Auditorium.... it just overwhelmed me to be where Hank Williams had stood so many years ago.

> —CLINT BLACK, making his Opry debut in 1989,
> almost exactly forty years after Williams
> had made his Opry debut

Jim Denny always sort of tried to run me off, because I didn't work the road. He was in charge of booking the artists [for road shows]. I was not productive to him, so I can understand his position. In later years, we became pretty good friends.

> —CHET ATKINS, quoted by the *Journal of Country Music,*
> regarding his early days on the Opry

Merle Haggard and Willie Nelson, his heart apparently mended, being honored in 1983 as the Country Music Association's Duo of the Year. (Photo provided by Lomax Photo Archives)

If you want to make a living with country music songs, stay away from Nashville. They'll just break your heart.

> —WILLIE NELSON, to Waylon Jennings, in 1965

You talk about a hen out of a coop—I really felt like one up there. I'm tellin' ya. But you know what? We made 'em show their true colors. We brought that country out of them if anybody did. They's sittin' up there stompin' their feet and yellin' just like a bunch of hillbillies, just like we do. And I was real surprised: Carnegie Hall is real fabulous, but, you know, it ain't as big as the Grand Ole Opry.

> —PATSY CLINE, to a concert audience in Atlanta

Even though I was not heavily involved in country music, the reason I came to WSM was the Grand Ole Opry. I thought the Opry made this radio station different from any other station in the country.

—HAL DURHAM, announcer

I thought to myself: That looks like fun down there onstage. And I thought if I ever finished writing this piece, I'd like to start a show like the Grand Ole Opry back in Minnesota.

—GARRISON KEILLOR, writing in 1974 for the *New Yorker*

The people would be watching for you. They'd be standing on the street corners and sidewalks.
—BILL MONROE, on the Opry's early traveling tent shows

I thought about Judge Hay that night, and if he were standing there giving me that advice [about loving the audience], it would have a great impact on me. That's what wisdom is. It's still alive fifty years later."
—CLINT BLACK

Country music has become more than a regional manifestation: it has become a national desire.
Newsweek, 1952

I knew about the Grand Ole Opry, and I listened to the Opry in those days [1932, he was twenty-nine years old]. Then, I started making an attempt to get on the Opry. It took me five years to get there. I'd come every year—two or three times a year—and try to get on. Their words were, "Sonny boy, we're filled up. Maybe someday we'll have an opening for you." Finally, that opening came, and I took advantage of it.

—ROY ACUFF

You know, everybody listened to that darned Grand Ole Opry. They took me and literally made me into a big name, and it was just because of the exposure on the Opry.

—FARON YOUNG

Faron Young was an Opry stage mainstay for many years, and had lots of friends away from the Opry as well. (Photo provided by Lomax Photo Archives)

Sam and Kirk McGee took me under their wing, and I was just always there. I would never have gone to college if Roy Acuff and Howdy Forester hadn't kicked my behind to do so. They were wonderful guys.... When I look back on those days, I realize Acuff was a pretty selfless guy to do that. So I went to Vanderbilt and then to MIT, and I guess you could say I did what they told me to do. And then I came back to play fiddle.

—WOODY PAUL, of the Riders in the Sky

Good afternoon, I work for the company that owns the Grand Ole Opry, and Roy Acuff asked me to come by and give you a personal hello. May I come in?

> —Opening line of the sales pitch used by National Life and Accident Insurance agents for many years

I thought, "This is the place we ought to be recording." It seemed to be the center of everything.

> —STEVE SHOLES, head of country music for RCA, on his first visit to the Opry in 1946

I ain't goin' to school always. I'll sing my song and make more money than any of you.

> —HANK WILLIAMS, to his family after quitting high school in the ninth grade

Who is that boy?
—UNCLE DAVE MACON, to Minnie Pearl regarding Hank
Williams, June 11, 1949, at the Ryman Auditorium

You know, you take milk, and cream will form at the top. And that's the Opry—the cream on the top.
—JUMPIN' BILL CARLISLE

My earliest memories of country music were sitting on my granddaddy's knee and listening to the Grand Ole Opry on Saturday nights. It was a magical, wonderful fairyland in the sky to me, like the air castle of the South.
—GEORGE HAMILTON IV, singer

George Hamilton IV long associated Saturday nights with the Grand Ole Opry.
(Joe Taylor Artist Agency photo provided by Lomax Photo Archives)

I was one of ten children, and we all sang and we all played music and we all learned to love country music from hearing the Opry.

—JEANNE PRUETT

I used to go to sleep on my grandfather's lap listening to the Grand Ole Opry in his Ford pickup truck out by the barn.

—RICKY SKAGGS

I like to remind the Nashville Area Chamber of Commerce that the Opry crowd is Nashville's biggest convention gathering of the year—and it happens every weekend.

—BUD WENDELL, Opry manager

I've thought many times if you sat down to design a successful show, you would probably do everything just the opposite of the way we do. I can't conceive of anybody setting out to pattern a show that has no rehearsals. And we don't know more than forty-eight hours in advance who is going to be here. We have no advance promotion of the artists you're going to see, and we continually interrupt the whole thing with commercials

—HAL DURHAM, Opry manager, talking about the magic of the Opry that drew capacity crowds for every show

The big tourist businesses that surround the Opry here would die if the Opry should stop operating. All the other things we've got in Nashville aren't big enough to keep the tourists coming.

—ROY ACUFF

It's like a kid growing up who wants to be a baseball player—in my era he wanted to play in Yankee Stadium. And for somebody who wanted to be in country music, the pinnacle, the top, the ultimate was the Grand Ole Opry.

—BILL ANDERSON, singer

On Saturday nights, when the Grand Ole Opry was on, we'd all gather around and watch the radio.

—WILLIE NELSON, country music legend

I had a musically religious experience. You hear of some people being born again spiritually; musically, I was born again.

—GEORGE HAMILTON IV, on how a night in the Opry audience made him abandon his already-successful pop singing career for country music

We played one date in Mississippi, and the people sat there with their shoes in their laps, the water was coming through there that bad. They's paddlin' their feet in that water, keeping time with the music.

—KIRK MCGEE, musician, on the enthusiasm of audiences
at the Opry's early traveling tent shows

I thought about Judge Hay that night, and if he were standing there giving me that advice, it would have a great impact on me. That's what wisdom is. It's still alive fifty years later.

—CLINT BLACK

CHAPTER FIVE

THE TRADITION

The debate over what makes the Opry the phenomenal success it is has often pitted tradition against innovation.

The focus in the beginning was the back-country music of the hill people. A star system soon developed, however, and the styles of individual performers became as important as the musical tradition.

As younger generations began to make their way into the Opry lineup, they often sought to incorporate elements they felt appealed to contemporary audiences. Older Opry veterans tended to consider such ideas sheer heresy. Such a dichotomy of styles has long graced the Grand Ole Opry, forming a potent mix of music that provides something for everyone—traditionalists as well as groundbreakers.

Elvis Presley's lone Opry performance was rejected as too unconventional. Tom T. Hall once quit the Opry because of its ban on horns. Tanya Tucker was once booed because her set was considered too close to rock 'n' roll.

Over time, the tension between the two camps tended to resolve itself in ways that did indeed reflect audience tastes. That was always the final word. Nothing ever survived at the Opry if it didn't strike home with the people in the seats.

Keep it close to the ground, boys.

—GEORGE HAY, first host of the WSM Barn Dance,
giving his signature admonition to
musicians new to the Opry

Country music don't change, fellows, it don't change.

—HERMAN CROOK, longtime Opry harmonica player,
on sticking to tradition

Whatever I was doing for a living, I'd just get tired of it. Music's the only thing I kept coming back to.

—ALAN JACKSON

You've always got to belong to somebody or something. Belonging to the Grand Ole Opry to me is like having a great support group at home always. No matter where you go worldwide to take country music where ever, you've got your support group back home and you've got a place to come to.

—JACK GREENE

There is no trick about it, and it requires no fancy key to open its front door. The latch-string is always out.

—GEORGE HAY, on the Opry's enduring appeal

Sometimes you never knew who might drop in, as Ernest Tubb (left) here meets up with Peter Fonda. (Alan Mayor photo provided by Lomax Photo Archives)

There are those who cross over the bridge and mix their music, but I personally have no desire to do this. Country music is good. It is humble and simple and honest and relaxed. It is a way of life. I like it, the people like it, and I'll stick to it.

—ERNEST TUBB

When we sang we sang of people and places that were familiar to us...we sang of problems—hard work, poverty, sorrow—problems that were part of our everyday life. We sang of hopes and prayers—that opportunity would come and free us from the hardships of our life, or that we would have a better home waiting in the sky.

—MAYBELLE CARTER

The sound is so much better today, with all the new technology. But you lose the spontaneity. There's something about a live performance in the studio. That's all we were doing. We didn't overdub, hardly ever. You get a different performance out of a singer if there's a pretty girl in the control room watching, and there's musicians all around that he's trying to impress.

—CHET ATKINS

There's nothing weird or complicated about the music we're trying to make. We're just cranking it up and going for a good time.

—KIX BROOKS, of Brooks and Dunn

It took a few years for Chet Atkins to prove to all the Opry man-
agers that he belonged onstage. (Columbia Records file photo
provided by Lomax Photo Archives)

Well, I'm going out there and do country music in my own way, just like I've always done it, and if they don't like me, I'll just come home.
—ROY ACUFF, commenting on his first Las Vegas engagement at the Showboat Casino in 1960

Just keep it country, son. Just keep it country.
—GEORGE JONES's advice to Alan Jackson

I'd rather ride a wagon and go to heaven than go to hell in an automobile.
—UNCLE DAVE MACON, banjo picker and first star of the WSM Barn Dance, who never learned to drive, and likewise felt there was no reason for the Opry to ever change

I don't know what it is. I think it's a state of mind. I don't think there's any danger of losing an identity.

—BILLY SHERRILL, record producer, in 1978 defining
the essence of country music

You need fiddles, guitars, banjos, and things like that. And play the old-time tunes and songs. That's what it's supposed to be.

—HERMAN CROOK

Being a member of the Grand Old Opry means that you've got a home as an entertainer when you're not on the road.... Not only that, you're a family. The Grand Ole Opry is still like the old days when the entire industry was like a family.

—JIMMY C. NEWMAN

Folks were not necessarily angry with me for singing the white's music. It was more curiosity than anything else. They were baffled. Its not like they wanted to beat me up or anything. It was like "How come you look like us but sound like them?" And for the whites, it was "How come you sound like us but look like them?"

—CHARLEY PRIDE

Charley Pride, one of the few blacks to make it big in country music, with the legendary Hank Williams looking over his shoulder. (RCA Records file photo provided by Lomax Photo Archives)

It's a religious event of sorts, sort of linking back to a tradition rich with history and meaning to all country music performers. And it extends way beyond the boundaries of Nashville—and our country. We have a Tuvan throat singer, Kongar-ol Ondar, whose one dream when he came to the U.S. was to play the Opry.

—JIM ED NORMAN, Warner/Reprise Nashville president

I got here at about the right time to be of assistance to the Opry. My group was strictly country-no electrical instruments, no horns, nothing except our own mountain way of presenting music.

—ROY ACUFF

Coming back to the Opry after time on the road is like a cool drink of water in July. It keeps you going.

—MARTY ROBBINS

Sam, that's purty, but it's too modern. What we want to do is keep the show down to earth.

—GEORGE HAY, telling Sam McGee not to play his electric guitar at the Opry

Roy Acuff said it would ruin the Opry forever. I wish I had a nickel for every time I heard something like that.

—MINNIE PEARL, referring to when Bob Wills's band played electric fiddles on stage for the first time at the Opry

When I was with Lester Flatt, it was an unwritten law that when you weren't on the road, you were at the Opry. It was like church—you didn't miss church. A lot of us don't go and play; the reason it continues to survive is the loyalty of the staples. Musically, it's in good shape, but as far as reverence and dedication, I don't know about that.

                       —MARTY STUART, on the future of the Opry

Marty Stuart gives to the community as well as to his Opry audiences. (Libby Leverett Crew photo provided by Lomax Photo Archives)

We were about the most surprised when they went to electrical instruments. We tried to bring 'em on before anybody. We brought an old National electric guitar we had, one night, and Judge Hay made us take it back. Said it was too modern to use on the Opry. Said we wanted to hold her down to earth. But it wasn't long after he was gone, they had one in every band.

—KIRK MCGEE, of the McGee Brothers, early Opry performers

I'd say that 75 percent of Hollywood is phony and maybe 25 percent is pure, whereas I'd say that our business here with the Grand Ole Opry is maybe 90 percent pure.

—ROY ACUFF

The Opry is really the centerpiece of Nashville's country music industry....The Opry is the great symbolic mother church that holds all of country music together.

—CHARLES K. WOLFE, Opry expert, Middle
Tennessee State University

Above all, we try to keep it homey. Home folks do the work of the world; they win the wars and raise the families. The Opry expresses the qualities which come from these people.

—GEORGE HAY

It's wonderful people aren't apologizing for country music anymore. I've always believed in country music and I have always done country music since the beginning of my career. And I always heard the line, "It's too country." To which I'd say, "That's what I do: country."

—EMMYLOU HARRIS

Emmylou Harris has cut a lot of great tunes, too. (Photo
provided by Lomax Photo Archives)

Edwin Craig wanted to keep the Opry the way it had been in 1935, with a cast made up primarily of instrumental string bands. He believed that the Elizabethan folk songs would survive, and he disagreed with the star system as it evolved.

—IRVING WAUGH

Irving Waugh started his long association with WSM and the Grand Ole Opry in 1941 as an early morning country music announcer for WSM. (Seiji Wada photo provided by Lomax Photo Archives)

They tried to make a New York show out of us and we won't change the Grand Ole Opry for anybody.

—ROY ACUFF, commenting on the failure of the Grand
Ole Opry as a summer replacement venue
at the Hotel Astor, New York City, 1952

I felt that you shouldn't restrict the Opry too much. You had to let it grow and take its natural course.

—JACK DEWITT, WSM president

You've got to have smelt a lot of mule manure before you can sing like a hillbilly.

—HANK WILLIAMS

You've got your hip country music, but out in the real world you have your cowboy stuff as well.

—JOHN JARVIS, country music keyboardist

When you leave the Grand Ole Opry, you should be able to say to yourself that you got some good out of it, that it was maybe like going to a good church service.

—ROY ACUFF

I'm really a country singer at heart. I don't try to categorize my music, but it's always been the same—real honky soul...It doesn't bother me to be labeled "country." Elvis was a country singer, so were the Everly Brothers. Those that think it's a problem are misinformed. I feel an obligation to carry on the music of my dad's time, the music of Hank Williams and Jimmie Rodgers. Their talents and their symbolism forged the style, and we draw upon a kind of universal storehouse of country music knowledge.

—RODNEY CROWELL

The Opry is like home.

—WILMA LEE COOPER, singer

It's time for the pawpaws to paw, the tall pines to pine, and the old cow to slip silently away.

—GEORGE HAY's closing words for many years
at the end of each Opry performance

You ask what makes our kind of music successful. I'll tell you. It can be explained in just one word: sincerity.

—HANK WILLIAMS

Eddy Arnold (left) and Archie Campbell enjoy a good laugh during a TV interview. (Photo provided by Lomax Photo Archives)

It was a real wrench to leave. I thanked the people for being so kind to me. Then I hurried off stage and cried in the wings.

—EDDY ARNOLD, on leaving the Opry

We didn't fire Hank (Williams, Sr.). We couldn't even find him.

—IRVING WAUGH, commenting on the widely held belief that Hank Williams was "fired" from the Grand Ole Opry

They were all nice to us out there, but it just is no place for us kind of folks.

—ROY ACUFF, upon returning to Tennessee from Hollywood after the filming of the 1940 movie Grand Ole Opry.

All the music training I ever had was from him. I was shinin' shoes, sellin' newspapers and followin' [this old black man] around to get him to teach me to play the guitar. I'd give him fifteen cents, or whatever I could get a-hold of for a lesson.

—HANK WILLIAMS, on Rufus Payne, "Tee-tot"

The Grand Ole Opry is as simple as sunshine.

—GEORGE HAY

Country music is American. It comes from the heart of America.

—PRESIDENT RICHARD NIXON, at the opening of the Grand Ole Opry House at Opryland USA, March 16, 1974

CHAPTER SIX

THE STARS

Instrumental music was the main feature in the early years of the Opry with the likes of Uncles Jimmy Thompson and Dave Macon. It wasn't long, however, before the star system began to creep into the show's essence, creating a recognizable worldwide phenomenon that today manifests itself in music videos built on marquee value and marketed with all the aplomb of Hollywood glitz-and-glitter machinery.

Soon after Roy Acuff first appeared on the Opry, in 1937, he had emerged as a star. It's no wonder: He sang with such feeling that he was known to cry during sad songs. He soon had big hits with "The Great Speckled Bird" and "Wabash Cannonball."

Ernest Tubb, a Jimmie Rodgers wannabe who had hit stardom with "I'm Walking the Floor Over You," joined the Opry in 1943. Other early stars followed, to include Eddy Arnold, Red Foley, and Bill Monroe.

Hank Williams Sr. made his debut on the Opry in 1949 with "Lovesick Blues" and was called out for six encores. His rousing popularity with Opry audiences has never been topped. Other stars came along in the 1950s: Hank Snow, Marty Robbins, Jim Reeves, Porter Wagoner, Kitty Wells, and Patsy Cline.

The sixties, seventies, and eighties would bring Loretta Lynn, Jack Greene, Dolly Parton, the Osborne Brothers, George Jones, Barbara Mandrell, John Conlee, and Emmylou Harris. The star system continued in the nineties, with contemporary performers such as Vince Gill, Joe Diffie, Lorrie Morgan, Marty Stuart, Martina McBride, and Garth Brooks.

Opry stars invariably have found themselves magnified into larger-than-life figures. They have shaped the image of the Opry as much with their personalities and lifestyles as with their music.

When I saw the Grand Ole Opry, the desire to be up on the stage with the performers was like a hunger.

—TAMMY WYNETTE

Tammy is still such an influence on women in music. I have been a fan, an admirer, tried to be a clone, and then became friends with her and really got to know the woman behind that great music.

—FAITH HILL, on Tammy Wynette

Now that we were Grand Ole Opry stars, I expected the whole world to change. It did.

—ROY ACUFF, on his soaring popularity after he and his band made their first Opry appearance

I don't read music and I'd fight the man who tried to teach me. I don't care whether I hit the right note or not. I'm not looking for perfection of delivery—thousands of singer have that. I'm looking for individuality. I phrase the way I want to. I sing the way I feel like singing at the moment.

—ERNEST TUBB

These country glamour boys are big—sometimes bigger in record sales and juke box popularity than Bing Crosby or Frank Sinatra. They live in mansions with swimming pools attached in Nashville's fashionable suburbs, drive immense automobiles bearing their initials in gold and wear expensive Western getups.

—*Nation's Business*, 1953

If I ever left the Opry, I'd have to fire myself.

—BILL MONROE

I can't understand a word he says.

—Frustrated substitute producer to Owen Bradley,
during a recording session with Bill Monroe

I think all my relatives own a Jerry Clower album.

—JEFF FOXWORTHY

Right now you're little darlins', but as soon as everybody knows you, after you've been successful for a number of years, that's when the industry is ready to write you off.

—MINNIE PEARL, to Randy Owens, member of Alabama

One of my strongest recollections, as a preadolescent sitting in the balcony, was the entrance of a young Dolly Parton onto that stage. I was immediately filled with great anticipation of the prospects of womanhood.

—AMY GRANT

[Backstage] People were picking and singing, and Vince [Gill] gave their [the Wilkinsons'] father a guitar, and they all played a song and blew everybody away. So, Vince said, "Let's go!" and he brought them out with him on stage to sing "I'm So Lonesome I Could Cry." Can you imagine? So many magical things happen at the Opry.

—TONY BROWN

Daddy took me to the old Ryman [in 1967], and we sat in the balcony and watched the show. And while I was watching I got the idea, "Hey, I can do that." I turned to Daddy and said, "I want to do that. I can't just sit out front here. I want to be up there."

—BARBARA MANDRELL

Once you've heard Barbara Mandrell sing, there's no question why she has won so many country music awards. (Photo provided by Lomax Photo Archives)

The credo "Two out of three
ain't bad" helped Garth Brooks make
it through the night at the Country Music
Association Awards in October 1991. After
winning top honors for Album, Single, and
Video of the Year, Brooks capped off the evening
by being named Entertainer of the Year. While
accepting that last trophy, Brooks paid homage
to two of his greatest inspirations: "My two
Georges; George Jones and George Strait."
Brooks then quickly added, "No offense,
Mr. President," referring to a third
prominent George seated in the
front row of the Opry House.
—President George Bush

Bill Monroe claims
he was late to the Opry only
three times in the more than fifty years
he performed there after joining in 1939:
once because of a flat tire, again when his
stretch limousine caught fire one hundred
miles outside Nashville, and when his
bus almost got washed off the road
in eastern Kentucky.

It's a long road. I'm delighted to be here.
—EDDY ARNOLD, upon accepting a nomination
into the Country Music Hall of Fame, 1966

I don't think it's so much what you sing, it's how you project it, how you make the audience understand the way you feel it.
—LORRIE MORGAN

Lorrie Morgan followed her father George's footsteps onto the Opry stage at an early age. (Photo provided by Lomax Photo Archives)

Red [Foley], he wanted me to be his sideman. He said, "I don't want you recordin' for other people, Ches. I want you to play with me." And I said, "Hell, I wanna be a star like you, Red."

—CHET ATKINS

The Grand Ole Opry is my life. And as far as I'm concerned, the Grand Ole Opry to the country music entertainer is like Hollywood to the actor, and I wouldn't trade my association with all these wonderful artists for anything in the world.

—LITTLE JIMMY DICKENS

Patsy stood there for a minute, then threw her head back and laughed a laugh that seemed to come from the soles of her feet. I just stood there dumbfounded. "You're alright, honey," she said. "Anyone that'll talk back to the Cline is alright. We're gonna be good friends." And from that moment on, we were. Patsy taught me something that night. If you expect to have friends, you have to be one.

—JAN HOWARD, recalling her introduction to Patsy Cline after performing at the Opry for the first time, and after Cline had lightly chastised Howard for not introducing herself earlier in the evening

I think I brought a different voice to the Opry. Most of the people on the show back then were crooners. They sang soft, and they sang harmony, where I would just open my mouth and fill my lungs with air, and let it go with force.

—ROY ACUFF

I always pray for patience. And I ask God if he can do it right away.

—BARBARA MANDRELL's favorite saying

Dottie and I were heading downtown in her Cadillac, but as usual, she was running late. We pulled up to the Opry's famous backstage door when the announcer on WSM said, "Ladies and gentlemen...here she is from McMinnville, Tennessee...." I'm seventeen years old; I've never been in the building....I'm freaking out....I'm running past Marty Robbins and Ernest Tubb, had no idea where I was going, where to plug in.... Later that night, it dawned on me. I just played the Grand Ole Opry!

—STEVE WARINER, then singing backup for Dottie West

We made that record ["Four Walls"], and he got right in the mike. When he sang "Four Walls," man, what a sound. I remember [record producer] Steve Sholes called me from New York and said, "How did you get that sound? How did you do it?"

—CHET ATKINS, marveling about Jim Reeves

Patsy Cline, Jim Reeves, and Grandpa Jones helped take the Opry to New York's Carnegie Hall in 1961. (Les Leverett photo)

Where else can you go and see Vince Gill play backup to Little Jimmy Dickens and sing harmony with him? Or Marty Stuart playing backup to Connie Smith and the White girls, doing that three-part harmony?

—BOB WHITTAKER

"That's kind of the way he drifted into that spot. Later on, that's the only show he would work. He didn't want to do anything else.

—HAL DURHAM, referring to Marty Robbins, whose burgeoning auto-racing career precluded him from performing Saturday nights at the Opry until the last segment that began at 11:30 P.M.

Elvis Presley was a country boy to start with and he just kinda put a swivel in his hip and did country music. I like to swing out, but I swing it from the heart. Presley swings it from the hip.
—ROY ACUFF, commenting on the impact of Elvis and rock 'n' roll on country music

Hanging out backstage in the dressing room with Carl Perkins and the Lonesome Cowboy band, listening to them swap stories—it was a great night, filled with old memories and ghosts of the past.
—JOE DIFFIE, recalling one of his first memories of the Ryman

It's still possible for new performers to make it in country music. But they have to come across in videos, and they have to be really sensational live performers.

—BILL CARTER, talent manager

When I sang that song ("Step Aside"), it sounded like Johnny Cash. If Roy Acuff would sing it, it would still sound like a Johnny Cash song. And you can tell when Nancy Sinatra sings it, that it's a Johnny Cash song.

—WAYLON JENNINGS

It's funny how a chubby kid can just be having fun and they call that entertainment.

—GARTH BROOKS

I never dreamed that I would be a part of that [the Grand Ole Opry].... It's a dreamland.... Probably the biggest shock of all was that these people treated me like I was some old war buddy.

—GARTH BROOKS, who says that his biggest thrill came when he was admitted to the Grand Old Opry

I went hungry a lot when I first came to town. When I got really desperate, I would go to Kroger or H. G. Hill's and push a cart around like I was shopping. I'd stop at the deli and pick up a sandwich, unwrap it and eat it, then leave the cart and go home! I'm not proud of that but, when I made it, I bought enough food from them to pay them back.

—DOLLY PARTON, on moving to Nashville
to make it in country music

Between the two of them, Clint Black and Dolly Parton have raised a lot of pulse rates among Opry audience members. (Photo provided by Lomax Photo Archives)

Although legendary hillbilly
blues singer Jimmie Rodgers, "the
Blue Yodeler" or "the Singing Brakeman,"
never joined the Opry, his influence on Opry
stars such as Hank Snow and Ernest Tubb was
indisputable. "I thought he [Rodgers] had his
own personal and peculiar style, and I thought
his yodel alone might spell success,"
said Ralph Peer, a record scout who
"discovered" Rodgers in 1927.

If Hank could raise up in that coffin, he'd say, "See, I told you I could draw more folks dead than you SOBs could alive."
—JIM DENNY, Opry manager, to Horace Logan at Hank's
funeral, attended by twenty thousand folks

He was just as authentic as rain.
—MINNIE PEARL, on why Hank Williams affected
Opry audiences like no other performer

The fans just didn't want to let him go. When Hank would work that stage, he would appear to be suspended in a blue haze.
—GRANT TURNER, announcer, on the electrifying
Opry performances of Hank Williams

He just seemed to hypnotize those people. It was simplicity, I guess. He brought his people with him. He put himself on their level.

—LITTLE JIMMY DICKENS, on Hank Williams's
unforgettable performances at the Opry

He was just a country hick like me.

—VIC McALPIN, Nashville songwriter, on Hank Williams

If it helps to take one pill every four hours, it must be even better to take four pills every one hour.

—HANK WILLIAMS

Hank Williams's light didn't burn long, but it sure burned brightly.
(Photo provided by Lomax Photo Archives)

I love this stage. You can let that curtain fly back and I'm ready.... It's just like when the whistle blows at a football game. You're nervous before it, but when the whistle blows, all nervousness stops and you're gone. And you forget about it, and you forget about your crowd and all....

—ROY ACUFF

I wonder why they don't like me at the Opry. Marty Robbins gets up there and does my songs, and they love him.

—ELVIS PRESLEY

Women in country music do sing about the bad side of life. And the way I handle that situation is that if I can sing about wife abuse, child abuse—anything like that, then hopefully someone in that situation will be able to talk about it—will have the strength to come out and talk about it and fix the situation.

—REBA MCENTIRE

I certainly never became one of the pack of cookie-cutter, stamped-out, here's-another-country-act in a cowboy hat.

—BILLY RAY CYRUS

It used to be that the old girl would say to her old man, "Let's go to the Opry," and he'd go reluctantly, because all he was going to get to listen to was old hairy-legged Ray Price, Roy Acuff, Marty Robbins and so on. But when it got to where these boy hillbilly fans could go and hear Kitty sing a love ballad, why naturally they were a lot more eager to go.

—JOHNNY WRIGHT, husband of Kitty Wells,
the Opry's first female superstar

Kitty Wells with another singing sensation, Marie Osmond. (Photo provided by Lomax Photo Archives)

This place'd hold a lot of hay.
—ERNEST TUBB, talking about Carnegie Hall, when a troupe
of Grand Ole Opry stars took the show to New York
for a 1947 performance

I've learned that money and the toys don't make
you happy.
—ALAN JACKSON

I'm an overnight success that took eight-and-a-
half years to happen.
—TRAVIS TRITT

It looks like maybe we're going under if you don't come back. Roy, you mean everything.

—HARRY STONE, program director, successfully urging
Roy Acuff to return a year after he stunned country
music by leaving the Opry in 1946

I went out to Hank's house and we tried, but I just couldn't write with him. I was so in awe of the man that I choked. I've still got fingerprints on my neck!

—CHET ATKINS, on his futile efforts to write songs
with Hank Williams

I saw Johnny Cash for the first time at the Opry. It was when he first came there.... That was also my first encounter with what sex appeal was. I was in the audience—I must have been ten or eleven—and I saw Johnny Cash, and I'll tell you, it was a feeling like I had never had before. I found out years later that what he had was called "charisma."

—DOLLY PARTON

Legendary Opry performer Stringbean. (Tennessee State Library and Archives)

CHAPTER SEVEN

THE FANS

On hot summer evenings and cold winter nights, the music spoke direct-
ly to the hearts of those who packed the wooden pews of the Ryman
Auditorium. It is not uncommon for visitors to remember exactly where
they sat and what they wore years ago, as well as who sang, who
played, and who told jokes.

They came in overalls and Sunday clothes, and in Fords and
Cadillacs and on the backs of flatbed trucks. They brought box lunches
of baked ham and fried chicken. Those who couldn't get tickets crowded around the open windows and peered inside.

America is a more affluent nation today, and, for the most part, so
are Opry audiences. They now enjoy the performances in the air-conditioned and roomier Opry House. Essentially, however, the same thing
keeps them coming back: The Opry is the ultimate in country music, and
the fans themselves are consummate lovers of music that is American in
its truest sense.

They sat on their hands sort of in awe. They would not applaud. Wild applause was a later development as the show became more famous, drawing people who were used to that sort of thing. No, the first audiences had the reserve of the real Anglo-Saxon type of people from the hills.

—AARON SHELTON, WSM engineer, on the original Opry audiences

What is more precious than being thanked by one of my all-time heroes ahead of his parents?

—"WORLD-FAMOUS" WAYNE REMENY, Nashville superfan, referring to George Hamilton IV's acknowledgment of Remeny in the liner notes of one of his CDs

They were hungry for the rhythm of the soil and the heart songs, plus the rural flavor and humor which spiced it.

—GEORGE HAY, on early fans at the WSM Barn Dance

Yes, it's a hard life, but I love it. I like one-night stands. I like meeting new audiences. I couldn't stand it if I had to keep on facing the same audience.

—ROY ACUFF, early in his career

They brought with them their chewing tobacco and gum and pocket knives to leave their initials in War Memorial's fine leather seats.

—GRANT TURNER, announcer, on the Opry audiences during its years at War Memorial Auditorium

Nobody liked us but the people. We didn't get much press coverage, and what there was, was not very complimentary. But I remember we got a pretty good response from the audience.
　　　　　　　—MINNIE PEARL, on the Carnegie Hall appearance

"My Fans Make Me a Happy Girl"
　　　　　　　Sign at Martina McBride's Fan Fair Booth, 1998

How-dee! Minnie Pearl, and a hello to you, too, Sarah Cannon—one and the same person. (Photos provided by Lomax Photo Archives)

If a fight ever breaks out when you're playing a honky-tonk, that first thing you should do is break into a version of "Silent Night." I've seen big old two-hundred-fifty-pound men stop fighting and break down and cry at that song. It's amazing.

—TRAVIS TRITT

When you listen to somebody's music over and over, you kind of feel like you know him. And then you come here and you meet him. It's almost like you feel you have a friendship.

—JULIE SBRACCIA, a fan from Boston

I'm so happy that people are here to see the show. And the problem I have is not being able to sleep after a show. I think it's because I get so excited, and I think about the show for a long time after it's over.

—MARTY ROBBINS

We never use the term hillbillies [when referring to Opry fans]. There is no such animal. Country people have a definite dignity of their own and a native shrewdness which enables them to hold their own in any company.

—GEORGE HAY

How important country music could be to these fans that they would wait for five hours just to get tickets! I can't express how I felt when I saw that happen.

—PORTER WAGONER, after seeing Opry fans lined up six abreast for blocks outside the Ryman at 6:30 in the morning

Audiences at the Grand Ole Opry are the most honest people in country music. Some of them will blow that smoke on you, tell you "Man, that's great," when you really don't think it is. You get a real honest response when you do something new at the Opry.

—PORTER WAGONER

Porter Wagoner has always pleased hordes of fans as a true country music rhinestone cowboy. (Photo provided by Lomax Photo Archives)

Allowing the audience to leave its seats to photograph and shake hands with the performers is a good indication of the Opry management's lack of concern for the balance of the paying customers. Were we glad that we hadn't paid big bucks to sit in the orchestra seats.

—HARRY AND JUNE PALMER, disgruntled Ontario, Canada, visitors to the Grand Ole Opry, in a letter to the newspaper

I do like to be able to play my songs. I'd have to say that if it never happened, I'd miss it, but when it does happen, I get a little distracted. I try to make a couple of jokes or re-sing a line that I missed because of it, and I think the audience gets a kick out of it.

—CLINT BLACK, referring to those rare occasions when he's "accosted" onstage by female fans

There are a lot of people there. Lots of pretty girls.
> —TOM RAULERSON, elderly Florida resident, in 1989 upon
> fulfilling a lifelong dream of visiting the Grand Ole Opry

Elvis didn't click at all on his first and only appearance. Our audience was there for dyed-in-the-wool country music, and that's not exactly what Elvis was doing.
> —LITTLE JIMMY DICKENS, on Elvis Presley's
> lone Opry performance

Just love 'em, honey, and they'll love you right back.
> —GEORGE HAY, to Minnie Pearl when she was
> a nervous Opry performer

An incredible intermingling of great national celebrity with rural and grass-roots citizenry. There's never been anything like it.

—PAT BOONE, on attending Opry shows as
a teenager growing up in Nashville

Be silly. That's what they pay to see. Turn loose, Minnie.

—ROY ACUFF, to Minnie Pearl in her early Opry days

An Opry audience can be as cold as a January night in Nome if a non-Opry member does an act they don't like.

—MINNIE PEARL

I'd like to walk around town or the mall with him. I'd say to my friends, "Hey, this is Hank." And everybody would be like, yeah, sure.

—ERIC VALENTINE, Virginia teenager, talking about his dream of one day meeting Hank Williams Jr.

Let's put the country back into country music, so that those same rural sounds heard seventy-five years ago, when Fiddlin' John Carson played "Little Log Cabin in the Lane," can be heard today in the sounds of newcomers playing on stations twenty-four hours a day and not just a few hours a week.

—WEBB WILLIAMS, a self-proclaimed "country music activist," in a letter to Bill Ivey at the Country Music Hall of Fame

Back in Maynardsville, Union County, where I'm from, we were considered hillbillies. We didn't resent it. We took it proudly, because there's nothing wrong with a hillbilly.

—ROY ACUFF

People love to cry.

—ROY ACUFF, after singing "Unloved and Unclaimed" at the Opry and being told it was too sad to be popular

Well, it didn't help her any.

—MINNIE PEARL's reply to questions about whether a fall hurt a woman who tumbled out of the Ryman balcony in her excitement upon seeing Bob Wills onstage

Don't get the big head, Clint. Their mammas used to do the same thing for me.

>   —ROY CLARK to Clint Black, referring to the young women
>   screaming for him at the taping of the Opry's
>   sixty-fifth anniversary show

I eat at her house every time I go to Nashville.... When she asked me to go with her to (an) autograph signing, I jumped up like a little doggie with his tail wagging.

>   —BART ORTIZ, Ohio rcountry music fan, commenting
>   on a friendship with Jeannie C. Riley
>   he built over the years

She can't remember my name, but she remembers my face. Barbara Mandrell has one of my pictures in her museum on display. I gave it to her in 1982.

—LORRI SADDLER, country music superfan from Jamestown, New York, who has had numerous photos taken of her with music celebrities

Barbara Mandrell hasn't let her high-flying career stand in the way of accessibility to her fans. (Photo provided by Lomax Photo Archives)

I'm a forty-something black woman who spent her youth in Washington, lip-synching to the Supremes and slow dancing to the Temptations. Now I often come home to my Manhattan apartment and put on Vince Gill, Randy Travis or Reba. Consider me a fan of country music. So there. Deal with it.

—LENA WILLIAMS, writing a "Pop View" column
in the *New York Times*

CHAPTER EIGHT

THE HARD TIMES

The Opry has known more than just limelight and applause. Changing tastes, generational differences, tragic accidents, societal pressures, and just plain ol' controversy have all created difficult times over the years.

But like a classic country song about overcoming adversity, the Opry has always kept on playing the music. The Opry endures in large part because even though it may have been knocked down, it never stayed down.

The Opry's staying power has become just one more facet of its legend and appeal. The individuals and families who follow country music can appreciate the way country's grandest institution continues to overcome its troubles.

In an age when so many traditions have fallen by the wayside, it is comforting to know the Grand Ole Opry continues to persevere.

Nashville, with all of its colleges and universities and high society, is a blue-blooded town, and for a long time the elite people in this city would have liked to see the Opry destroyed and done away with.

—ROY ACUFF

I remember especially one Saturday night. It was a Christmas Eve. There was hardly anybody there in the Ryman Auditorium. Some of the best shows were during the holidays when all the stars were home in Nashville. But that night nobody came to see them.

—GRANT TURNER, announcer, on the 1950s period
when television, air conditioning, and rock and roll
depressed Opry attendance for several years

The Opry didn't have the appeal to the younger audience that you have to have if you're going to keep growing. All I could see there were older people and little teeny kids. There weren't any teenagers.

—DEE KILPATRICK, on problems he faced when named manager of the Opry in 1956

Steve didn't understand the kind of stuff I ought to do, and he'd bring these things that I just couldn't do at all. I just lost interest. He brought in one time a thing called "Hey Liberace." It was ridiculous, and I told him so. I said, "I can't do that stuff." I don't think he liked it too well. I got the ax pretty soon after that.

—GRANDPA JONES, referring to Steve Sholes, his producer at Victor and an architect of "the Nashville Sound"

I took the mike stand, threw it down, then dragged it along the edge of the stage, popping fifty or sixty footlights. The broken glass shattered all over the stage and into the audience. The song ended abruptly, and I walked offstage and came face to face with the Grand Ole Opry manager (Ott Devine). He kindly and quickly informed me, "We can't use you on the Opry anymore, John."

—JOHNNY CASH, writing in his autobiography
about his drug-use days in 1965

Johnny Cash and George Jones offer some in-your-face country music. (Beth Gwinn photo provided by Lomax Photo Archives)

Branson made Nashville wake up.

—PAM TILLIS

Fear doesn't come from God. Fear comes from Satan, so when you're afraid, don't cry out to God, rail at Satan.

—GENE MILLER, Barbara Mandrell's friend, giving her some advice before her 1986 comeback after suffering injuries sustained in a car wreck in 1984

Ya'll don't worry, 'cause it ain't gonna be all right nohow.

—HANK WILLIAMS, on pessimists

Those guys aren't doing anything except making records with a little heavier beat and singing
some pretty good songs. Guys like Willie and
Waylon are doing a fine job. Heck, I've known
Waylon for years and those guys aren't doing
anything but helping this business. Maybe their
lifestyle is something else—letting their hair
grow long, skipping a couple of baths and puff-
ing that stuff—but their music is fine.

—EDDY ARNOLD, 1976, regarding the "outlaw"
country music genre of that era

The child labor laws were strong at that time [early 1940s]. The authorities kept putting restrictions on WSM about what they could do and could not do with us, and it got to be a little too much for the Opry management. After six months we had to leave.

—TEDDY WILBURN, of the Wilburn Children

They would want us to keep smiling and to recall the happier occasions. I feel that I can speak for all of them when I say let's continue in the tradition of the Grand Ole Opry.

—OTT DEVINE, then the Opry manager, concluding a moment of silent prayer at the first Opry performance after Patsy Cline, Cowboy Copas, and Hawkshaw Hawkins were killed in a plane crash in March 1963

I have a feeling we are losing so many of the old-time musicians, the old-time comics, that we've already turned the corner. I know that tastes are changing, a lot of the younger fans don't understand the country idiom, the expressions from the soil, that are contained in some of the best of the old songs.

—GRANT TURNER, Opry announcer

Let's forget about the accident. I'm not an invalid.

—ROY ACUFF, walking with a cane at his first Opry appearance two months after a near-fatal automobile accident

If it hadn't been for the Opry in the first place, none of the country stations would be where they are today. I have no ax to grind; in fact, I've only performed at the Opry once in my life. But that's where my country roots are. Back in the old days, when there was no other medium but WSM and the Grand Ole Opry, there was hardly another station in the world playing country.

—CONWAY TWITTY, responding in 1978 to criticism leveled
by other stations' disk jockeys at his newly released song
"The Grandest Lady of Them All," because the song
was about a rival station, WSM, home
of the Grand Ole Opry.

Loretta Lynn and Conway Twitty performing an impromptu rehearsal. (Photo provided by Lomax Photo Archives)

I had so many things I was going to say tonight. I want to thank all my friends for their concern, and I want to thank God for letting me be here. Now I can't think of anything to say, so I guess I'll have to sing for you.

—MARTY ROBBINS, upon returning to play a packed house at the Opry after a massive heart attack a year earlier

Hank Williams got kicked off the Opry for drinkin' too much old wine. Me, I got kicked off for singing about the new wine.

—SKEETER DAVIS, after being dismissed for expressing support for Vietnam War protesters during an appearance on the Opry

There was a period in the history of the Opry when it was felt that the Opry probably would not survive. That's a well-known fact in music circles but probably not outside.

—BUD WENDELL, referring to the fifties

I think we have finally convinced the greater part of the Nashville elite people that they were mistaken in thinking that the Opry should have been kicked out and put somewhere else, like back into the mountains. I believe the majority admire us now for the determination we've shown here.

—ROY ACUFF

He had decided it was time for him to make his move. Either they [WSM] put Flatt and Scruggs on his half hour of the Opry or he would pull his company's advertising off the station. So they allowed the boys to work the Martha White show, but they were still not considered members of the Opry.

—JAKE LAMBERT, Lester Flatt's biographer, referring to Martha White Flour's Cohen Williams, pulling strings to keep Flatt and Earl Scruggs on the Opry schedule, allegedly against the wishes of the duo's former bandmate Bill Monroe

CHAPTER NINE

OPRYLAND

National Life broke ground in 1970 on Opryland USA—a theme park northeast of downtown Nashville, along the Cumberland River—as the new home of the Opry. Although there was talk of tearing down the Ryman after the Opry moved to Opryland in 1974, public outcry convinced the powers-that-be that the building should stay, so it was renovated and remains one of Nashville's most-frequented tourist attractions. Today, music once again fills the old Ryman, with artists worldwide performing on its legendary stage.

In its first six months at Opryland, the Opry surpassed its record annual attendance figure set during its last full year at the Ryman.

On July 1, 1983, Gaylord Broadcasting purchased Opryland USA, including the Nashville Network (TNN), which had just been launched a few months earlier. It would broadcast the Opry and an array of other country programming from studios at Opryland USA.

Declining attendance and revenues, however, forced Gaylord in 1997 to announce it was closing the Opryland theme park, which was to be replaced 2000 with Opry Mills, a large shopping mall built with an entertainment premise expected to sustain and further grow tourist traffic to the Opry House. The two-year lag between the closing of Opryland USA and the opening of Opry Mills resulted in a further downswing in Nashville tourism, although the Grand Ole Opry continues to live on and thrive as a country music institution that might just last forever.

Opryland USA will be the site of WSM's famous new Grand Ole Opry House. This great American show has become a national institution. The new Opry house will still be under construction when the park opens. When it is completed, it will be the nation's largest radio and television studio, seating forty-four hundred visitors.

—Opryland U.S. press release, circa 1972

I shocked a lot of people when I took the stand that the Opry should move to the new Opryland. I hated to think about leaving the old building, but, I'll tell you, I worried every Saturday night. That old building was going to fall in someday.

—ROY ACUFF

Let 'er go, boys!
    —ROY ACUFF, using a favorite phrase of the late George Hay
        to kick off groundbreaking for construction
            on Opryland USA in 1970

I don't know what anyone is so upset over leaving tradition at the Ryman. The Opry had five homes before it ever wound up there. It didn't lose any flavor when it moved before. It won't now.

    —BUD WENDELL, Opry manager

Bud Wendell. (Photo provided by Lomax Photo Archives)

And then when they told me about how that circle in the middle of the stage came from the old Ryman Auditorium, I could really feel the history and the emotion that all the Opry members share.

—CLINT BACK

That's one thing they should have thought about before they moved us out of the Ryman. They lost their sales on all them hand fans when they moved out to an air-conditioned building.

—JUMPIN' BILL CARLISLE

It just had more personality.
>   —GRANDPA JONES, comparing the Ryman to the
>   new Opry House at Opryland USA

Unlike other major theme parks, Opryland USA presents the authenticity and uniqueness of America rather than its fantasy.
>   —Opryland USA press release

Our distinction in the theme park industry is the number and variety of musical stage productions we present.
>   —JULIO PIERPAOLI, Opryland general manager

Prior to the park, the only reason to come to Nashville was to go to the Grand Ole Opry. What the park began to do was create a destination attraction that we needed. It gave people a reason to stay and legitimized Nashville as a vacation destination.

—BUTCH SPYRIDON, Nashville Conventions and Visitors Bureau

Opryland was looking for something that was an alternative to music.

—BOB EUBANKS, game-show host, explaining why he brought his "$25,000 Game Show" to Opryland

Well, in this professional company, I'm a little embarrassed to try and play that thing there.

—PRESIDENT RICHARD NIXON before consenting to
Roy Acuff's request that he play the piano
at the opening of Opryland USA

I've had some tough acts to follow in my career, but this is unreal. I wouldn't wish a spot like this on a dry cleaner.

—JAN HOWARD, singer, following Nixon's
enthusiastically received appearance

Someone was telling me that there is only one thing stronger than country moonshine, and that is country music.

—RICHARD NIXON, at the opening of the
Grand Ole Opry House

That was one of the high spots in my life.... to have the privilege of meeting Richard Nixon on the stage and introducing him to the nation. It's something not every country boy has had the opportunity of doing.... and I still think he was a great president.

—ROY ACUFF, describing the 1974 visit of
Richard Nixon to the Opry House.

The Opry has survived because it's been an ever-evolving entity.

—BOB WHITTAKER

I can remember when that curtain came down. Well, we were going from what we knew and loved and held dear to the unknown. And I just wondered to myself if it was the end of the Opry, or was it the beginning?

—JEANNE PRUETT, after performing in the last
Grand Ole Opry show at the Ryman

I've heard some artists say, "Well, the new house is not the Opry." But to me, the Opry is the people, not the brick and stone.

—JAN HOWARD, on the move from the Ryman
Auditorium to Opryland USA

Jan Howard has seen the Opry through the days of the Ryman and, most recently, Opryland. (Photo provided by Lomax Photo Archives)

We have memories here [at the Ryman]. Some good, some punishment. And the punishment is making folks come to a place like this. You have to pay a dollar for a fan and buy a cushion to sit on. At the new Opry House, we'll do the fannin' and give you music, as well.

—ROY ACUFF

It's hard to put a finger on it, but it seems to me that in the past five years or so there's been a renewed interest in the Opry by the Nashville "establishment."... The latest crop of young stars really seems to revere the Opry more than we've seen in past years.

—KYLE CANTRELL, Opry announcer, in 1998

The Grand Ole Opry House is our center-piece—our castle. And for the first time ever, we will create the internal access and position of prominence the Opry House deserves.
—TERRY LONDON, president and CEO, Gaylord

For the next five years, we have a lot of things on the drawing board. New shows, physical changes. It's safe to say we won't stand still.
—CHUCK BUCKNER, Opryland general manager, in 1996

It looks to me like they're more or less standing still.

—TOM POWELL, *Amusement Business,* commenting on
the modest changes made at the Opryland
theme park for the 1997 season

Our park, while having the rides, has always been known as a musical park. Music is the point of difference. It is the heart of American music.

—JACK VAUGHN, president, Opryland Hospitality
and Attractions Group

I think the Gaylord people are smart enough to realize you can't just raise attendance quickly by changing shows.... You have to bring in an $8-10 million roller coaster.

—TIM O'BRIEN, *Amusement Business*

Opryland, to put it bluntly, is a dull theme park. The Gaylord ideal has been to downplay rides and focus on live entertainment. As a result, you get few thrills and lots of musicians pretending to be someone else. And once you've seen an Opryland show, you've seen it. There's no reason to go back.

—TOM ROLAND, *The Tennessean*

There is always nostalgia for things lost, but institutions are always reinventing themselves. I would far rather see them change than to let the park get worse and worse.

—PHIL BREDESON, Nashville mayor, after it was announced in 1997 that the Opryland theme park would be closed and eventually replaced by Opry Mills

This was a 100-year-old carousel in the middle of the water at Opryland. (Photo courtesy of Country Music Hall of Fame)

It's been a good, safe venue for families to go to for entertainment. I'd hate to see anything change that wholesome atmosphere.

—KEVIN GREEN, Nashville visitor to Opryland

I do feel like the park will be gravely missed, especially by the season-ticket holders. The park has been a wonderful opportunity in my life. It has afforded me the opportunity to get off the road. It's not that seven-day-a-week grind any-more.

—JEANNE PRUETT, Opry member

Once you've done Opryland, that's it. Now, shopping, is a different story.

—DONNA WALTERS, Knoxville resident and Opryland
theme park tourist, reacting to news about the
impending construction of Opry Mills

The Opry is the raison d'être for the whole attraction out there. Whatever they do or do not put around the Opry, it will be around and thriving.

—ED BENSON, executive director, Country Music Association

I hope it's a whole new rebirth of everything out there. If they do make the Grand Ole Opry the center of it all, so much the better. Because that is why the country fans come to Nashville.... The main thing they come here to see is the Grand Ole Opry. And never, ever lose sight of that.

—JEANNE PRUETT

SOURCES

Billboard.

Country Music Hall of Fame and Museum.

Cross, Wilbur, and Michael Kosser, *The Conway Twitty Story.* Garden City, New York: Doubleday and Company, 1986.

Fortune.

Fremont (Ohio) *News Messenger.*

Hagan, Chet, *Grand Ole Opry.* New York: Holt and Company, 1989.

Jamestown (New York) *Post-Journal.*

Journal of Country Music.

Kingsbury, Paul, *The Grand Ole Opry History of Country Music.* New York: Villard Books, 1995.

Nashville Banner

Nashville Business Advantage

Nashville Business Journal

Roanoke (Virginia) *Times and World News.*

The Ryman Remembers: Recipes and Collections, the Ryman Auditorium. Nashville: FRP, 1996.

Tassin, Myron, and Jerry Henderson, *Fifty Years at the Grand Ole Opry.* Gretna, Louisiana: Pelican Publishing, 1975.

The Tennessean.

Tucker, William L., *Face to Face with Country.* Branson, Missouri, and Tucker, Georgia: Branson Publishing, 1994.

U.S. News and World Report.

Washington Post.

Wolfe, Charles K., *The Grand Ole Opry: The Early Years, 1925–35.* London: Old Time Music, 1975.

About the Editor

Randall Bedwell is the author of more than a dozen books about the Civil War and Southern history. His works include *Brink of Destruction*, the seven-volume *May I Quote You, General?* series, *Christmas in the South*, and *General Lee and Santa Claus*.

A veteran publisher and author, he is president of History Village, Inc., which produces limited edition lighted porcelain replicas of historic buildings for historical societies, churches, and preservation groups throughout the United States. He and his wife, Amanda, and their son, John Riley, live in their hometown of Paris, Tennessee.

Printed in the USA
CPSIA information can be obtained
at www.ICGtesting.com
JSHW052016140824
68134JS00027B/2506